The End Is Just The
Beginning

"A cook book but not what it seems"
Tragedy, Triumph, Success!

SCERENA THOMPSON

To order additional copies of this book, contact:
Xlibris
AU TFN: 1 800 844 927 (Toll Free inside Australia)
AU Local: 0283 108 187 (+61 2 8310 8187 from outside Australia)
www.xlibris.com.au
Orders@Xlibris.com.au

ISBN: Softcover   978-1-6641-0148-7
        EBook   978-1-6641-0149-4

Print information available on the last page

Rev. date: 10/30/2020

The end is only the beginning

I have been set a challenge to write my memoir accompanied with a cookbook. But not just any cookbook one with my personal struggles which has included weight, dyslexia, juggling a 13-year-old and ten-week-old premature baby. Additional challenges have included trying to move forward with my business and progress as a successful caterer with my company The Leading Tailored Cook, and also living in Sydney without immediate help. Don't get me wrong, help is a phone call away in the next state and we are blessed as a family that I have my mother to take Mayson (my 13-year-old) every school holiday's. Above all, keeping emotions in check and trying not to fall over in heap and just start crying uncontrollably.

Along my path of self-discovery, I have met some amazing people. People who read this book may not think they are anything but they have inspired me to keep going no matter how many obstacles I face, no matter how many times I fall on the cement and graze myself. Those are the people who I look up to in this book and is dedicated to them.

My father, may he Rest in peace, was a pillar of strength when I needed him the most. There was a time when it was dark and he got me through it made sure I was okay. My grandmother called him the back bone of the family and he was. When he found out I was pregnant with my first child, he was on the edge of the bed and I heard this 'Thud' on the floor. I said, "Dad are you okay" and he got up abruptly and said "I'm fine", "I'm fine". He was just in shock and I didn't find out about this until a couple of years after he passed away that this had happened.

My mother, who is the calm after the storm, has comforted me when I needed her the most. We have become quite close over the years. She always used to say to me "You are so much like your father" and I used to respond, "I am my father". When I told her I was pregnant with Decoeta she was at work and she was entering a lift. She stopped dead in her tracks and the doors didn't close. My mother had said "What,

what was that" and I told her "mother you're going to be a grandmother again" my mother's response was "oh right okay", completely in shock.

My husband, who is my strength and my partner-in-crime, when I had none, inspired me to keep going when I thought I couldn't. He took care of my child when I couldn't, even after I got out of hospital, when I got discharged from hospital he said "You have been in here for 11 days" my reaction was "Oh my God, I feel like I've been in this cult, with the heavy tranquillising tablets I was on for my High Blood Pressure. I said "let's get out here" as I had not realised I was in there for that long. It took me another 6 weeks for me recover.

My grandmother (Mimi) is stealthy in beauty and strength. When you are around her, you feel at ease with her. My Grandmother has been through a lot of her own personal battles with health however she always comes out the end smiling, and has this tenacity to keep going no matter what life throws at her, and no matter how many challenges she must face. I think that's the way I look at life sometimes no matter how hard I fall I get back up and do it again.

All vegan and vegetarian recipes here.

1. Vegan Brownies

Almond milk	1 cup
Coconut sugar	½ cup
Plain flour	1 cup
Cocoa powder	½ cup
Baking powder	1tsp
Slat	½ tsp
Dark chocolate chips	350grms

Method

1. Put oven to 160*C and line square tin
2. Add milk, cocoa powder, baking powder, salt into a bowl
3. Sift flour in bowl
4. Add melted chocolate and mix with a paddle on low speed
5. Put in tin bake for 20mins

2. Potato Rosti

Potato	200-300grms
Plain flour	50grms
Egg replacement	Directions of use are on the package 1 tsp for one whole egg
Powder	1tsp
Mushrooms	100grms
Onion	1

Method

1. Peel potato, cut, boil in a saucepan let them cool down in the fridge
2. Cut onion fry in pan along with the mushrooms then put to the side
3. Mash potato add in salt, pepper, plain flour, egg replacement powder
4. Divide potato 4 balls then roll out
5. In a large fry pan cook on both side
6. Put in onion, mushrooms and roll
7. Eat and enjoySpinach Handful

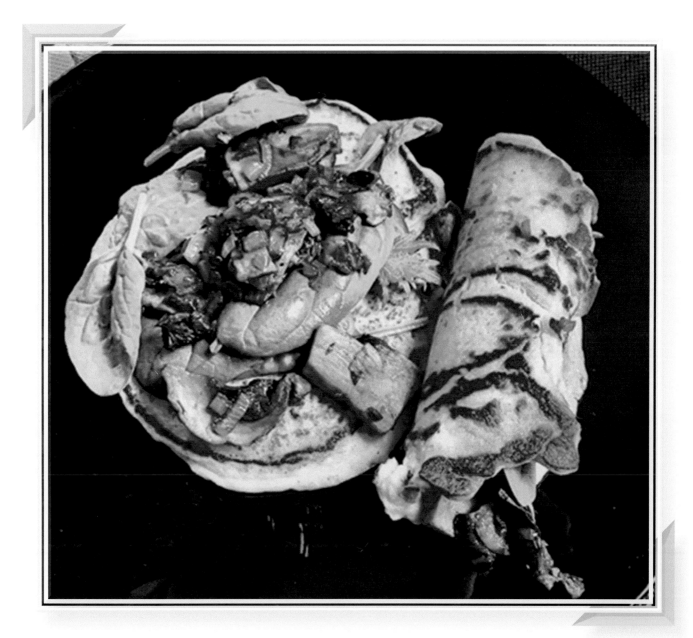

3. Creamy Coconut Pumpkin Soup

Pumpkin	1 (butter nut personal preference but you can use any!)
Coconut cream	1 tin
Paprika	½ tsp
Vegetable stock	50mls

Method

1. Peel, cut, boil pumpkin in a saucepan
2. Drain water mash pumpkin
3. In a clean saucepan return to heat add coconut cream, paprika, vegetable stock, salt pepper heat serves

4. Vegan Pizza

Cauliflower	1 head	Powder	2 tsp
Salt/ pepper	1 pinch of both	Onion	1
Garlic	2tsp	Mushrooms	200grms
Parsley	1 bunch	Vegan cheese	100grms (grated)
Rosemary	1bunch	Capsicum	1
Plain flour	50 – 100grms	Spinach	50grms
Egg replacement	Follow directions on package	Tomato paste	4 tbsp

Method

1. Clean, cut, boil Cauliflower let cool down then blend in a blender
2. put oven 160*C
3. put blended cauliflower into a bowl along with egg replacement, 1tsp garlic, plain flour, ½ rosemary, ½ parsley, salt, pepper
4. Mix until its dough you may need to add more flour if need be
5. Get a tray spray on oil baking paper roll out the pizza dough to the tray size   Bake for 20 mins take out turn over bake for a further 10 mins
6. Chop vegetable and lightly cook them put them to the side put the rest of the herbs in the vegetables
7. Grate cheese
8. Put tomato paste on pizza base
9. Put cheese toppings on pizza base
10. Put back in oven and cook until cheese is melted

5. Vegetable bean salad

Black beans	1 tin
Fava beans	300grms
Zucchini	1
Baby Eggplant	1
Onion	1
Capsicum	1
Mushrooms	100grms
Zatar	1tsp
Garlic	2tsp
Thymus citriodorus	2tsp
Parsley	½ bunch

Method

1. Soak beans in water over night
2. Cut up vegetables any way you like
3. Drain beans
4. Put spices and in a frypan with a little oil
5. Put vegetables in onion being the first to cook it down make it translucent then add the rest mushrooms being the last
6. Put beans in cook them
7. Get a bowl toss parley little olive oil salt pepper then you're done

6. Vegetarian bean burrito

Kidney beans	1 tin	Olives	1 small jar
Spanish onion	1	Pitta bread wrap	1
Mushrooms	100grms	Salt/pepper	1 pinch
Capsicum	1 (you pick colour)	Lemon grass	1 stalk
Tomato	1 tin	Chilli	1
Zucchini	1	Garlic	3 cloves
Spinach leaves	150grms	Parsley	½ bunch
Rice	100grms		

Method

1. Soak beans over night
2. Cut all vegetables any way you like
3. Cook rice
4. Cut herbs when it comes to lemon grass turn your back of the knife over hit the hard-wooden end with back of knife.
5. Put in fry pan all herbs expect for parsley with a little oil
6. Put vegetables in and cook except mushroom and spinach
7. Drain rice
8. Put parsley, spinach, mushroom, tin of tomato, olives in fry pan
9. Salt/pepper
10. Put rice in pan
11. Heat through put into wrap, wrap up bread and enjoy

7. Vegan Power pack balls

Peanut butter	1tbsp
Dates	10
Cocoa powder	1tbsp
Coconut	30grms
Water	100mls

Method

1. Put everything in the blender and blend
2. Get a container and roll them into balls put them in
3. When rolling make sure you have wet hands store for 2 months in fridge
4. Let it set in the fridge for 1 hour
5. If the mixture is too wet little trick put some oats or breadcrumbs into mix.

8. Coconut Vegan Cookies

Coconut	80grms
Nutlex butter	100grms
Plain flour	150grms
Almond Milk	5tsp
Baking powder	1tsp
White sugar	50grms
Vanilla essence	2tsp

Method

1. Get a bowl put in sugar, Nutlex and cream together
2. Put in almond milk, vanilla essence and mix
3. Put in baking powder, coconut and mix
4. Put in flour and mix
5. Roll in clean film into a log put in freezer overnight
6. Next day turn oven to 160*C
7. Take out of freezer cut with a serrated knife 1-2cm in thickness
8. Then bake for 15-20mins or until golden brown

9. Vegetarian Gnocchi

Potato	1	Vegetable stock cube	1
Capsicum	1	Almond milk	30mls
Mushrooms	200grms	Nutlex	30grms
Onion	1	Parsley	½ bunch
Carrot	1	Zatar	1tsp
Zucchini	1	Lemon pepper	1tsp
Flour	50grms		

Method

1. Boil potato in a saucepan filled with water
2. Chop up all vegetables any way you like and put to the side
3. Take potato off pierce with a fork if it goes through without resistance potato is ready to come off the stove drain and mash.
4. Mash potato put butter, milk, ½ quantity of flour make sure you can roll potato into little balls that's how you know you have added enough flour
5. Roll into balls put to the side
6. Heat up pot of water until boil
7. Cook vegetables put to side in the oven to keep warm
8. Put herbs and spices in the potato and flour as well make a dough and roll into little balls and put to the side but while you are doing that get a pot fill with water and once you have finish rolling the potato into little balls the water should come to the boil and put in and wait until balls come to float on top that how you know they are ready.
9. With the stock cube put in pot and water and flour to thicken up to make a sauce.
     Drain Gnocchi grab a bowl put Gnocchi, vegetable sauce eats and enjoy.

10. Vegetarian rice with veggies and creamy coconut sauce.

Capsicum	1
Mushrooms	200grms
Onion	1
Carrot	1
Zucchini	1
Eggplant	¼
Broccolini	2
Parsley	½ bunch
Zatar	1tsp
Lemon pepper	1tsp
Chilli	1
Garlic	3 cloves
Coconut cream	1 tin
Rice	½ cup

Method

1. Get a pot of water let it come to the boil
2. Chop all vegetables any way you like
3. Cook rice for 30 – 40 mins depending on the grain or until you think rice is cooked
4. Drain rice put the side
5. Let herbs and spices infuse in the fry pan with a little oil except for parsley
6. Cook vegetables in a fry pan
7. Add salt and pepper
8. Put cream coconut in
9. Let it simmer for further 5 mins
10. Eat and enjoy

Decoeta born 19/12/2018
1.435kg Time: 6:15pm
Picture of her in her first hours of being born

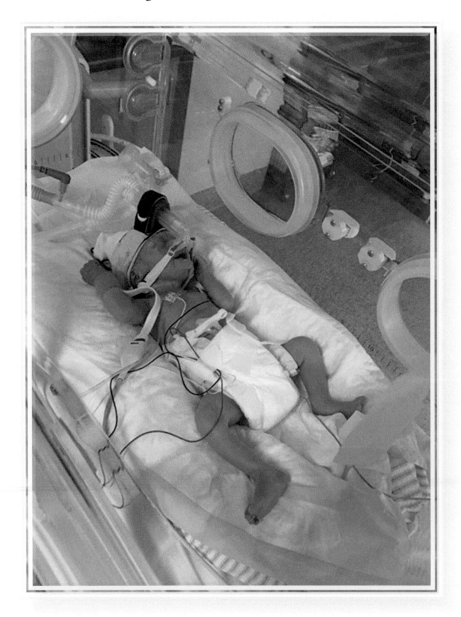

Decoeta is coming home today from ICU
Date 13/2/2019

I think when I was 15, I had a really good hard look in the mirror and it looked back at me. I could see a reflection of myself but add on 15 years. You never want to face the enviable that is going to happen to you if you continue down a certain path. It was scary and confronting at the same time but I also knew it was going to happen. When you're overweight and you have dyslexia, people at school can tease you, they can put you down so very harshly. When you have dyslexia, it's ten times worse. My mother always used to say "You can count your best friends on one hand" and "the definition of a best friend is they call you just as much as you call them" I was very naïve didn't think everyone was my best friend but I was craving friends and wanted to be accepted. I wanted to belong to a group or to something. When you're young, even though I was the eldest of four, I envied my sister's friendships with her friends. You tend to think why can't I have that too? I ended up making real friendships in my late 20's I never told my parents how much it affected me, but I think deep down she always knew. So after the 8ᵗʰ grade, my parents did the best thing for me and pulled me out of school and put me straight into home schooling I was so happy no one teasing me no one was calling me names like "you're so fat", "you could be a pork chop", the rest I really don't remember because I have blocked it out but it was enough for me later on in life for me to develop an eating disorder where I spent one year throwing up everything I ate. After a year, I thought this isn't for me, I love food then I went the other way I became obese, disgustingly obese, then when at time went on I lost my son to DOC's, I tried to kill myself. I was a single mother who didn't know what to do. I sat on the front porch of where I was living at the time and I rocked for two hours saying to myself "this is all a bad dream, it's not real, and he will come back" but he never did! I was damaged, "I was broken." And four years didn't feel like a mother I was ashamed, and dead inside of whom I was, and who I've become. Had a friend, who went through the same thing as I and said "Your child came out of you? Did he not" Then you are his mother. No matter if the law takes your rights away, No matter if your family doesn't talk to you, you are still his biological mother even now as I write this I willow up inside sometimes I'm still that little girl who sits on the porch all those many years ago. I had just spilt from my husband who abused me for four years everyway you could possibly envision "I was broken" and now I got what I wanted which I was a no body and that's how I wanted to stay. Then when they found out I have dyslexia the teasing got worse to the point where I became an emotional eater something went wrong so, I turned to food for comfort. I used to get up in the middle of the night and just eat because I was distraught. The only thing that was familiar was food, food wasn't going to judge me, and food wasn't going to tell me I was fat. I used to think food was better off in my stomach than sharing between everyone else. It took me somewhat years to have a good relationship with food sometimes even now I struggle. Some people turn to music, some people turn to drugs/alcohol for me it was food, food was my comfort. The entire emotional trauma that I endured I have blocked a lot out for a reason. My psychologist said to me "with all the emotional trauma you went through you should be in a psychotic ward"

Stop Hold on Decoeta smiled
9/3/2019

From a very young age, I always knew that I wasn't accepted anywhere and that was okay I'm different. In school when my parents paid for my sister and myself to go to Garden Angles we were there for a total of 6 weeks and the Principal of the school called my parents in to the office and said "Your daughter Tamara can stay but your daughter Scerena can't" Apparently I made the school look bad because I was under performing". That really didn't sit well with my parents. I already had the struggles with dyslexia I didn't really need the struggles of where to go to school as well. It was harsh back then. Dyslexia was not recognised back in the early 80's as it is now. Now at the age of 37, it's different you just accept and move on. My sisters and my brother always told me I was adopted because I was so vastly different from them in the way how I act, think, and felt. Even as an adult today, process, comprehend I look like my father and have the hearing of Nini my Great Grandmother. Apparently, I have the Russell gene and find it hard to lose weight and keep it off. It's partly gene related but a massive amount depends on what you eat. I didn't know then what I knew I always felt lost didn't know my way through life at a very young age you were taught to have a career and get a job don't be such a screw up. I knew what I wanted to do however it just took me a while to get there. To follow my head, my heart, and stop listening to people saying that "I couldn't do it", "You're such a screw up. You'll never be able to make it". All that negativity weighs you down after a while, it's like you're in a pool of words and everyday your fighting to get through them. You're screaming from the inside out at the top of your lungs, no one looks up to notice you. That's what's it's been like for me for years with my schooling with weight then you have these hurdles these barriers if you will these mountains seems too great to climb. One day.......

I'm sitting up by myself
9/5/2019.

Beef Recipes

Osso Bucco

Beef Osso Bucco	1 each	Honey	1 tbsp
Diced tomatoes tin	1	Corn flour	20 mls
Garlic Cloves	1-6	Water	30 mls
Rosemary	1 bunch	Butter	30grms
Thyme	1 bunch	Milk	10mls
Sage	1 bunch	Slat/Pepper	pinch
Potatoes	1 per person		
Baby Carrots	1 bunch or depending on how many people		
Baby Broccoli	1 bunch or depending on how many people		

Method

1. Preheat oven to 100*C
2. Chop garlic, get a fry pan put the garlic, with a little oil tin tomatoes, and fry off simmer for 3 mins
3. Chop all herbs put to the side
4. Put Osso Bucco in a deep tray along with herbs cover with foil put in oven cook for 6 hours
5. Top and tail carrot, peel potatoes and put in the pot
6. Drain pot remove carrots and put to the side
7. With the potatoes mash put butter, milk, slat/pepper and mash keep warm
8. Cut ¼ off the stems on baby broccoli
9. Get a fry pan put in honey, little salt/peeper, baby broccoli, carrots, water let it warm through and toss it.
10. They should be soft to touch and falling off the bone that's how you know it's ready
11. Take out the Osso Bucco put to the side keep warm
12. Put the sauce in a pot with corn flour let it thicken up
13. Grab a plate and serve

Beef Stir – Fry

Onion	1		Sauce:	
Capsicum	1		Dates	1 hand full
Carrot	1		Garlic	4 cloves
Zucchini	½		Mixed spice	5 grms
Mushroom	50 grams		Ground Cloves	5grms
Strips of Beef	20 grams		Pine Nuts	Hand full
Bochy	1		Lemon	½ Juice
Rice	1 cup (does 4 people).		Water	25 mls

Method:

1. Put sauce ingredients in a blender and blend then put to the side
2. Cook rice this will take 20 minutes
3. Cut veggies anyway you like set aside you want to cook the hard veggies first to ensure that you don't overcook the soft veggies
4. Little bit of oil in a fry – pan or a wok let it heat up
5. Put hard veggies in first let cook for 2 – 3 minutes or translucent in texture
6. Put in soft veggies cook 1 minute
7. Put in strips of beef let them cook and add in sauce at the same time

Beef Tacos

Taco mix:

Beef mince	1KG
Onion	1
Capsicum	1
Mushrooms	300grms
Taco shells	1 packet or depending on how many you have in your family

Sauce:

Garlic	5
Tins of tomatoes	2
Tomato paste	150gms
Onion	1
Salt/pepper	Pinch
Use a bit of taco seasoning	

Salad:

Lettuce or spinach	1
Cheese	depending on how many people you have in your family
Tomato	depending on how many people you have in your family
Onion	1 (optional)

Method

Mince:

1. Cut the onion and capsicum any way you like
2. Cook vegetables
3. Then pre – heat oven to the directions on the packet
4. Brown mince spoon out fat
5. Put mince in the vegetables then put to the side

Sauce:
(Napoletana)

1. Put onion and garlic in with a little oil and cook
2. Put in the tomato paste to be cooked off
3. Add tin of tomato's and let simmer for 5 mins
4. Salt/pepper for taste
5. At this point add sauce to the mince then let reduce this could take up to 1 hour but very nice.

Salad:

1. Put salad together in a bowl be creative.

Beef strips on an open sandwich with garden salad

Ingredients

Beef strips	20 grms
Tomato	½
Lettuce or spinach	hand full
Cheese	1 slice
Avocado	½
Slice of bread	1

Method

1. Gill the beef strips and cut to the desired way you want (mine is Medium Rare) then let it rest.
2. Get the slice of bread and put it in the oven to melt the cheese @ 50*C
3. Cut tomato, avocado any way you like
4. Assemble and enjoy

Spaghetti

			Sauce (Napoletana)	
Beef mince	1KG		Garlic	5
Onion	1		Tins of tomatoes	2
Capsicum	1		Tomato paste	150gms
Mushrooms	300grms		Onion	1
Spaghetti pasta	20 grms for one person		Salt/pepper	Pinch
			Use a bit of taco seasoning	

Method

Make the sauce first
1. Get a pot put garlic and onions and sweat them down
2. Put the tomato paste in cook it out
3. Put the tins of tomatoes and put them in let it simmer for 5 mins and you're done with the sauce.

The beef mince
1. Get another pot fill with water pot it on until boil
2. Get a pot sweat down the onion
3. Add in capsicum then the mince
4. Take out the fat if you wish
5. Add in mushrooms and sauce
6. Cook until the sauce has reduced you want to leave a little bit in there because when you heat back up after refrigeration.
7. Cook pasta for what every instruction say on the packet.
8. Eat and enjoy

Lasagne

Beef mince	2KG
Onion	1
Capsicum	1
Mushrooms	300grms
Lasagne sheets	1 packet 2 at most depending on how many layers

Sauce
(Napoletana)

Garlic	5
Tins of tomatoes	2
Tomato paste	150gms
Onion	1
Salt/pepper	Pinch
Use a bit of taco seasoning	

(Cheese Sauce)

Butter	20 grms
Flour	30 grms
Milk	300 mls
Cheese grated	300 grms

Make the sauce first

1. Get a pot put garlic and onions and sweat them down
2. Put the tomato paste in cook it out
3. Put the tins of tomatoes and put them in let it simmer for 5 mins and you're done with the sauce. Put to the side for later

Cheese Sauce

4. Get a pot put butter in let it melt
5. Put the flour in cook it out by whisking it you want to make white roux with the butter and flour whisk until combined
6. When you add the milk add the cheese bit by bit
7. Add milk 100 grms at a time whisk until it becomes thick repeat process until all milk is used then put to the side to use for later
8. Put oven on to 160*C or as advised by instructions on the packet of Lasagne sheets

The beef mince

9. Get another pot fill with water pot it on until boil
10. Get a pot sweat down the onion
11. Add in capsicum then the mince
12. Take out the fat if you wish
13. Add in mushrooms and sauce
14. Cook until the sauce has reduced you want to leave a little bit in there because when you heat back up after refrigeration.
15. Cook pasta for what every instruction say on the packet.

Assembly

16. Get out a deep square wide tray
17. Mince, then lasagna sheet, then cheese sauce
18. Repeat process I do about 3 layers
19. Put in oven for 35 – 40 mins or as advised by instructions on the packet.

Warm Beef salad

Broccoli	1-2 stalks	**Sauce**	
Spinach	handful	Garlic	5 cloves
Beef strips	20 grms	Parsley	½ bunch
Asparagus	1-2 stalks	Turmeric	pinch
Avocado	¼	Lemon pepper	pinch
Onion	¼	Golden syrup	10grms
		Apple cider	5 mls
		Worcestershire sauce	5 mls
		Sesame seeds	5 grms
		Corn flour	10grms
		Water	15 mls

Method

1. get a pot fill it with water wait until it comes to the boil
2. In the meantime cut Woodie ends off asparagus
3. Cut all the other vegetables any way you like
4. Cook onion, beef strips (frypan) broccoli, asparagus (boil) until ½ soft then take out drain put to the side
5. Get a bowl put all ingredients for the salad in then put to the side

Sauce
6. Put everything into a blender except for corn flour and water
7. Get a cup but corn flour and water in and mix
8. Then get a pot then let it come to a simmer and put in corn flour and whisk until sauce thickens

Then get a steel bowl put all ingredient in toss sauce through and then put in a serving bowl eat and enjoy.

Beef rissoles with vegetable

Beef mince	500gms
Onion	1
Carrot	1
Spring onions	2
Potato	1 for one person
Slat/pepper	pinch
Flour	10grms
Eggs	1
Chili powder	5grms
Milk	10mls for one person each additional person get put 5mls
Butter	15grms
Bread crumbs	20grms

Sauce

Garlic	5 cloves
Pine nuts	hand full
Dates	hand full
Water	25 mls
Zarate	5grms
Lemon pepper	5grms
Water	20 mls

Method

1. Get a pot boil potatoes once done drain and put to the side
2. Cut the onion any way you like and the spring onion
3. Get your mince, onion, carrot, (great carrot) chili powder, bread crumbs, salt/pepper, flour, egg put into a bowl and mix until well combined
4. Wet your hands roll mince mixture into balls weighing about 50grms each
5. You can fry rissoles in a frypan or you can put rissoles in a oven 100*C for 10 mins up to you
6. Get the potatoes and prepare the mash but in butter, milk, salt/pepper, onion put to the side but keep warm
7. Put the sauce into a blender and blend
8. Get a small pot heat until warm stir occasionally
9. Then put on the plate and eat

Sloppy joes with baked sweet potato chips

Mince	1KG		**Extras:**	
Carrot	1 (grated)		Cucumber	4 (slices)
Onion	1 (chopped)		Tomato	3 (slices)
Turmeric	pinch		Chips	hand full
Chili powder	pinch			
Garlic	5 cloves			
Bread crumbs	20gms			
Plain flour	30grms			
Egg	2 (Fried, mixture)			
Sourdough bun	1			
Spinach	hand full			
Onion	¼ (sliced)			
Mushroom	hand full			
Cheese	1 (slice)			

Method

1. Cook chips as per instructions on the packet
2. Pre heat oven to 100*C
3. Get a bowl add mince, carrot, onion, turmeric, chili powder, garlic, bread crumbs, plain flour, egg mix until well combined roll out 30 grms of meat into a beef Pattie
4. Get a fry pan cook onion, mushrooms, egg then put to the side
5. Add a little oil cook the beef Pattie put to the side
6. Get your bun slice in half, put the cheese on, put it on a tray into the oven until the cheese has melted
7. Cut up the extras if you wish assemble and enjoy

Spicy Italian meat balls with green vegetables and mushroom sauce

		Sauce:	
Mince	1KG	Dates	4
Carrot	1 (grated)	Garlic	5 cloves
Onion	1 (chopped)	Mushrooms	300grms
Turmeric	pinch	Water	200 grms
Chili powder	pinch		
Lemon pepper	pinch		
Garlic	5 cloves		
Bread crumbs	30gms		
Plain flour	30grms		
Egg	1 (mixture)		
Beans	10grms		
Asparagus	3		
Zucchini	½		

Method:

1. Get a bowl add mince, carrot, onion, turmeric, chili powder, garlic, bread crumbs, plain flour, egg, lemon pepper mix until well combined roll out 15grms of meat per ball then Lightly fry in a pan and put in the deep dish covered with foil in the oven at 50*C let them cook while preparing vegetables (put oil on the bottom so they don't stick)
2. Get a pot fill with water and allow it to come to the boil
3. Meanwhile prepare beans, asparagus, zucchini (cut zucchini any way you like, top and tail beans means cut off both ends, asparagus take off woody end meaning cut ¼ ends off)
4. Sauce put all ingredients into a blender then blend and get a sauce pan heat up slowly

Grilled beef stripes with char grilled vegetables

Eggplant	½ whole one
Pumpkin	¼ of a butter nut
Beetroot	3 slices
Chat potato	1 cut into slices
Beef strips	100grms for one person
Garlic	3 cloves
Juice of a lemon	1
Sweet honey soya-sauce	5grms
Paprika	5grms
Salt/ Pepper	pinch each

Method:

1. Marinate meat with lemon juice, garlic, sweet honey soya – sauce paprika, salt/pepper then put to the side
2. Put oven on fan forced 50*C
3. Cut eggplant, pumpkin, beetroot, chat potato
4. Use a skillet for the char grill marks or if you have a BBQ or a grill use that salt/pepper vegetables and cook them up they get the char grill marks
5. Get a tray put vegetables on a tray and cover with foil put it oven and let them still keep warm
6. Get a fry pan cook the meat
7. Take your vegetables out serve on a plate eat and enjoy

I had a middle aged crisis, well what I call a "Man Crisis". I just stopped listening to all the people that brought me down all the people that told me "I wasn't good enough" "I was never going to make it" all that pent up anger, I got rid of all of it. I started to live for me I felt so liberated I felt alive I felt free, I had nothing to lose but fear itself. By walking up to the highest peak in Sydney and shouting at the top of my lungs and getting a few looks from people. I shouted, "I Deserve Everything" And at that exact moment, my whole world had to change and from that moment, everything did. I put my fears aside and went for a career that I felt suited me. My personality, my passions, my inner desire to change. So I thought of a career I was most passionate about in my professional career and always go went back to. For me, becoming a chef. I went through many positions as quickly as a new pair of underwear. I would get through the first stage of the interview, then the trial was very good at then stayed for 4 months then they turned around would and say "Oh we don't want you working here anymore". It was the norm and it was a way of life. For me, food was a way of bringing families together and the very reason I became a chef was when I put a plate of food down in front of a person, I wanted them to enjoy it as much as I enjoyed cooking it for them and that's where it all began. It didn't end despite me being a single mother, overweight and dyslexic. I, took myself through an apprenticeship, got my qualification and became one of the success stories. I stuck to my guns and despite my mother always calling me "Stubborn" at the age of 33 finished (started when I was 30). Nothing could stop me. Nothing ever has. What I've learnt along the way about food has been nothing but incredible, when I first started, I thought this is it I have hit the jackpot. It was hard work but I was determined and, prepared to put in the time, effort, and the hours. Yes, I was a lot older than the previous apprentices that have walked through those doors so the employers always asked me "Why do you want to be a chef". My response was "I have passion, hunger to learn and, I can do anything." Now being overweight and a chef, the embarrassment set in at my first place I worked as an apprentice. When I was asked to get something for the Head Chef and I couldn't fit through the narrow path so he got it for me and didn't make too big of a deal out it but all the years of emotional eating had taken its toll on me and it's not because I would eat unhealthy. I would eat too much, not enough exercise and eating at irregular hours which all contributed to being overweight. Yes, this book is about honesty so me being honest with myself I would have the occasional couple of slices of pizza, or a whole pizza to myself but I don't need to tell you what makes you overweight you know for yourself and your experience. In the first year of my apprenticeship, I was Sexually and, physically abused at a company whom I had worked for (not naming which one) but my thinking was who would want to do that to an overweight person, who would want to like me or like my body or bluntly putting it 'who would want to get their rocks off with me' I'd dealt with a lot previously, already way more to deal with before I felt right in the head so to speak, the head chef threw a Lemon pie at the side of head he had told me "It's my fault he drinks "V" I turned around and said "you choose to drink "V" you choose to put that drink in your hand, put it up to your mouth, open your mouth and drink it, not me." It was then I stood up for myself where as I couldn't before. When I was abused by my ex-husband, I didn't have the strength or the guts to. However that day I stood up to my head chef and it felt bloody good. My ex-husband abused me badly for 4 years. I don't remember much as I have blocked most of it out, the mind is a strange and powerful I because of the abuse I'd suffered I wake up every night from nightmares however I've come a long way since that day mentally and physically so this is why I had the guts to stand up to my ex-boss and ex-head chef. My manager took me a-side and said it was my fault he was acting the way he was. Then I had said "No it's not, he chooses to act like this, and I want it to stop." At that point, I'd lost my job for standing up for myself and for being outspoken but I didn't care. Before I left I left them a little present, a little parting gift if you will, a dead rat at the back of the van and a phone call from the health inspectors the very next day said they had to shut down heard got word from a very good friend of mine that they never re – opened their business. It was a finished bit devious but well worth it to call anonymously. It was sweet, sweet revenge and I still believe to this day they still deserved it. That was my first year of being an apprentice but I, never quit once I had a goal and, I had to complete it, and I did!

Today I am 4 months, I start my first solid! 16/5/2019.

Picture of her very first solid.

Bare all naked truth so, 7 years have passed now, and I am pregnant my thoughts were WTF it has been 14 years since I've had a child. My husband and I were not trying to fall pregnant, it just happened, so we told my mum. She was working at Sarina Rosso at the time and she was heading into a lift and she stopped dead in her tracks. The doors were about to close and she could not move. She told my grandmother, my other grandmother and my grandfather. They were happy for me along with both of my sisters and brother. They were happy for me to tell Pat who is Craig's mum. She said "excuse while I pick my jaw up." Craig's sister on the other hand Katrina is a talker and you can't get a word in edge wise, shut up for the first time. You couldn't even hear a pin drop. Both brothers (on Craig's side) and Gran congratulated us. For the first two months, didn't even know I was pregnant, as I was working at the time and one day I finished work then got my first massive migraine which put me in bed for three days. I stopped at Broadway shopping centre, walked past the fish shop three shops down and I could still smell the fish I went up to a complete stranger and said "can you smell the fish"? They said "NO" then I walked off! I got a test at Colese, went down stairs, took the test looked at it then screamed at the top of my lungs "HOLLY SHIT" in a bathroom full of people. I called my friend but couldn't speak so I walked back home and sat at the front of my place for two hours then when Mayson had went to bed I told Craig and his response was "Well you got what you wanted then" I was eight weeks pregnant, two months had went by and I didn't even know. I wasn't trying because my doctor had said "Because of the excessive weight gain, you can't fall pregnant anyway" Due to me being at 130 KG before the pregnancy, throughout my pregnancy I suffered from health problems such as Gestational Diabetes, High Blood Pressure and because of the HBP, I had Migraines. It was never what I ate that was the problem. It was purely my portion size which I don't think I could ever get that under control. Reason being working odd hours and the sheer number of people I'd being catering for, finding out I was pregnant, there was never an easy moment I'd had a chat with my husband saying if this was deformed in any way I would terminate. I don't think Craig and I would have survived our marriage if she had of been deformed with so many babies with having deformity one way or another, I didn't want to be responsible for bringing another child into the world like that. Going to the antenatal clinic once every fortnight because I was categorized as a high risk, you tend to feel like a cattle number rather than a person, I had a lot of fear from my last pregnancy being pregnant at 22 though it is a lot different than being pregnant at 37. There are so many more health risks involved because I was already at 130KG. If I didn't have her early and they didn't give me the injections to speed up the lung capacity development neither she or I would be here today telling my story. With two months of my pregnancy left I gave birth to a little girl. It wasn't my diabetes that put me in hospital; it was my HBP due to me being so over - weight to begin. With my highest being 160 over 100, they tried everything all the medication under the sun then one day it spiked to 200 over 100 then my sugars flat-lined to 1 went into diabetic coma. I'm in the hospital and had 20 doctors and nurses around me. I came to and didn't know what had happened. I knew I didn't feel right felt dizzy then just passed out. I went to sleep luckily and had enough strength to get up into bed. At that point, I didn't know what was going to happen; I just didn't know how quickly it was going to happen. All throughout my pregnancy I knew how sick I was however I've always had that fire inside of me just to keep going and I know that someone is always looking out for me, maybe my dad which I had hoped! Maybe my guardian angel, always no matter what happened to me, no matter how sick I became I was going to be OK! I thought like that because if I didn't, I would just end up in a heap in a fetal position on the floor crying all the time. The pregnancy was hard and had a lot of stress that contributed to my HBP and also the stress fear of my first pregnancy. I'd try so hard to separate the two but you must! I gave birth to a little girl on December 19, 2018. 1.413KG at 6pm with my husband by my side. Earlier on that day, I had called my husband and said they are going to take the baby, via C-section it's time. My first reaction was trying to organise Mayson because he couldn't be in the delivery room with us. He was reluctant to do anything that I had suggested so his first words were "you haven't even asked me if I was going to be in the delivery room with you" my reaction was "are f******ing kidding me,?! I shouldn't be asking you whether or not you want to be there, you should just be here. You're the one who helped create this person living inside me, and I have to ask you whether or not you are going to be here?, You have one hour to be here or we are done!" I was more prepared to have a "C section" this time around than the first time. When I was attending the antenatal appointments, they weren't going to do it but I'd had pushed for it then having the stress to deal with the fact that my baby was in ICU and I couldn't take her home like a normal parent could after 5 days in hospital, I went home she couldn't. Sobbing for weeks on end because I couldn't have her in my arms, the only way I could hold her was when she was attached to leads and watching her take a breath wondering whether she was going to stop breathing and, on two separate occasions she did. I watched her take her last breath and I was there in the room when all the alarms with all the leads she was attached to, I performed CPR then watched anxiously as the nurse took over it was the most terrifying moment of my life. She was in ICU for two months and never left her side. Not only that, my mother called me up and said she had breast cancer. It was like deja vu all over again, my father had died a month before my son was born then this directly one month after my daughter was born a tragedy happens in the family. That was hard. I couldn't speak to my mother so I had to shut her out to deal with it and fell into a heap and started to cry. Moving forward she is fighting it and she is cancer free now. Eight months have gone by now and she is healthy and fit doing so well. When it came to breast feeding, that was a whole different experience. She wouldn't have a bar of me so the nurse said "she has created an aversion to me" meaning that she for some reason or another she was afraid of me just didn't want to breastfeed. What the nurse really meant is she has developed a fear of the boob. Oh well, so I expressed for 3 months every 3 hourly just to keep my supplies up. I was exhausted so to put a comical spin on things there was a time where Craig was regiment to feeding and he thought that if she was fed more than 2 times in 1 hour in a half, that it was called over feeding so here how it went.

Here is Decoeta speaking to her Daddy at 2am this morning here is her stomach;

Decoeta: I'm hungry

Stomach: Feed me

Decoeta: I'm hungry, I'm going to make your life a living Hell if you don't feed me!

Stomach: Feed me.

Decoeta: I'm hangry

Stomach: Feed me NOW.

Craig Thompson defence: "Oh I don't want to over feed her".

Me (Mother): Feed her NOW!

When it came to my weight I've tried everything to lose it every diet you could possibly imagine Weight watchers, Jenny Craig, Lite and Easy, Atkins diet, Cabbage Soup diet where you would eat nothing but spicy cabbage soup I did lose the weight but I was taking drastic measures to do so then I'd put the weight back on and a little extra. Let's face it we've all been there right? So this is why I've decided to take drastic measures to control my weight permanently so I have decided to go through the process of having a Gastric Sleeve done. During the pregnancy I ballooned up to 150KG so you can imagine me being the height I am which is 5'1 or 151cm at 150KG I found it really hard to breath and walk. I couldn't even talk without losing breath but bear in mind; I was pregnant at the time. Also, my right foot when I was pregnant when walking, I was walking on the side of my foot not flat. My feelings at the time was I'm so overweight if I put on anymore, I'm going to be bed ridden and to get this baby out of me but I'm sure if you're pregnant you feel like that anyway? My weight before the operation was 127kg and now my current weight is 107kg and still dropping. Ever since after the operation, I really haven't had an appetite to eat. Sure I miss it but the doctor had taken out literally ¾ of my stomach. The doctor said do you want to keep it? No, why?

So, here is me at 150kg. At a size 26. Picture. When I was pregnant

So now at 107kg with no appetite it has taught me a couple of things. I have to completely do a big overhaul and rethink the way I look at food, not using food as an emotional tool but rather to use food as fuel for the body to survive. It's like the doctor has taken away the desire for me to eat. It was an emotional adjustment as well you have to completely change the way how you look at food. So the 6 weeks leading up to the operation I had to go on a shake diet to teach me that one day. I'll be able to eat like everyone else but it will always have to be modified so a small is in fact an extra small portion but what is good about that is once I drop a dress size I won't put it back on or so I thought my sister on the other hand has gone for the same operation as me and she put back on 15KG. You can stretch it if you over-ate and have to have the mentality of, if you feel full that's it, don't eat anymore. She was full but then she would throw it back up and then wait ½ hour then start eating again. When I do come off the shakes, what was really good about it is I was allowed to have anything liquid so I could have spinach and carrot, celery and water any combination could think of and that would give me the energy I was lacking.

Here is me at size 24.

Day of the operation August 6, 2019. 5:30pm the day my life had changed forever! I went in there at 12:30pm the guy before had complications so that made me a little worried the nurse say to me "You don't have to worry all you have to do is just sleep and you're all done. Wake up and that's it" it's like thanks; I've just heard that there were complications with the previous patient and you're telling me not worry, Yeah right! I was thankful they gave me relaxant to calm me down before I went into theatre at that point; I had a migraine and was petrified but didn't have to worry! So, the surgery went well and I live to tell the tail.

Here is me at a size 22.

The day after surgery all I wanted to do is hold Decoeta, that was it and see my son Mayson and Craig. I felt confident that I would beat this weight gain once and for all, optimistic I couldn't eat but that was okay, it was so painful even to drink water. I had to learn how to drink slowly one cup took me ½ hour to drink, but I was on a free fluids diet for 6 weeks pretty much trying here and there to introduce solids back in. Being naughty I was just so sick and tired of the shakes because I was on them 6 weeks before hand so when I got out I still had to be on them but it taught me that I had to sip slowly so for the first 2 weeks free fluids, weeks 2-4 puree food and weeks 4-6 mush the nutritionist says to me "you can have a steak and blitz it" I was craving food because of my profession but I really wasn't hungry I looked at her and I said "I'm sorry that is not happening". What a waste of a perfectly good stake! You must have your protein and you need energy. So I went away thought about it and thought you know what after the six weeks if I still don't feel like eating I can always go back to the shakes during the day and have the one meal at night that's what I've been doing and I am still dropping weight I am in a size 18 now and back to what I was a couple of years ago. I think the most things I was worried about is coffee and alcohol. If they took that away from me. I don't think I could function or be me I mean come on now they took away ¾ of my stomach and even it has been 7 weeks after surgery they have taken the ability away from me to have a sandwich. I can't even have bread because it swells up in my stomach and to get through a ¼ of a sandwich, I have to give it away.

Here is me at a size 20.

Had decided to have the surgery even before I got pregnant didn't know she was literally going to change my life told my surgeon he said "well would have preferred you had the surgery then got pregnant" "Now we'll have to wait" My response was didn't know I was pregnant.

Chicken Recipes

Slow cooked chicken burger

Chicken Mince	1KG		
Carrot	1 (grated)		
Onion	1 (chopped)		
Turmeric	pinch		
Chili powder	pinch		
Garlic	5 cloves		
Bread crumbs	20gms		
Plain flour	30grms		
Egg	2 (Fried, mixture)		
Sourdough bun	1		
Spinach	hand full		
Onion	¼ (sliced)		
Mushroom	hand full		
Cheese	1 (slice)		

Extras:

Cucumber	4 (slices)
Tomato	3 (slices)

Method:

1. Get a bowl add mince, carrot, onion, turmeric, chili powder, garlic, bread crumbs, plain flour, egg mix until well combined roll out 30 grms of meat into a beef Pattie
2. Get a fry pan cook onion, mushrooms, egg then put to the side
3. Add a little oil cook the beef Pattie put to the side
4. Get your bun slice in half, put the cheese on, put it on a tray into the oven until the cheese has melted
5. Cut up the extras if you wish assemble and enjoy

Slow cooked soft chicken tacos

Chicken breast	2-3 depending on the people in your family
Thyme	1 bunch
Rosemary	1 bunch
Garlic	5 cloves
Zatar	2 Tbsp
Cheese grated	200grms depending on the how many people in your family
Tomato	1-2 depending on the how many people in your family
Lettuce	200grms depending on the how many people in your family
Onion	1
Soft tacos shells	1 packet
Mushrooms	200grms
Capsicum	1

Method:

1. Preheat oven to temperature on the packet for the soft taco shells follow directions for cooking times
2. Slow cook chicken by getting the slow cooker put with water then add thyme, rosemary, garlic, zatar for 1 hour then shared and get a fry pan on low heat put the liquid in and let it evaporate and stir occasionally
3. Cook onion, capsicum, mushrooms put to the side
4. Cut up tomato put to the side
5. Great cheese put to the side
6. Assemble and serve

Chicken stir-fry with rice

Chicken breast	1-4
Onion	1
Shallots	1 bunch
Capsicum	1-2
Carrot	1-2
Mushroom	300grms
Rice	250grms
Water	400mls
Ginger	10grms
Garlic	5 cloves
Honey	20grms
Mustard	15grms
Macadamia Nuts	2 handfuls

Method:

1. Get pot for the rice and cook the rice for 20 mins once water is boiling
2. Cut chicken breast and fry off with salt/pepper and put to the side
3. Cut onion, shallots, capsicum, carrot in a fry pan put to the side
4. Then Mushrooms, ginger, garlic, honey, mustard, macadamia nuts put into pan cook the mushrooms then add chicken, and vegetables back in mix all together
5. Strain rice
6. And serve

Apricot chicken with rice

Chicken breast	1-4
Broccoli	1- 2 heads
Shallots	1 bunch
Onion	1
Carrots	½ per person
Sage	1 bunch
Oregano	1 bunch
Apricots	300grms
Water	400mls
Butter	20grms
Salt/pepper	pinch

Method:

1. Put the chicken breast in a pot of water with a stock cube and let simmer for 15 mins or until chicken is cook put to the side
2. Cut onion, carrot, shallots, brocoli fry them in a fry pan put in the oven to keep warm
3. Put Sage, Oregano, Apricots, water in a blender and blend put in a small pot and heat up slowly
4. Cut chicken breast and put the mash, and vegetables on the plate and enjoy

Char grilled chicken skewers with apple rocket salad

Chicken breast	1-4 depending on the size of your family	**Salad:**	
		Walnuts	2 Handful
Garlic	2-4 cloves	Rocket	500grms
Lemon juice	10 mls	Pumpkin	300grms
Salt/ pepper	pinch	Apples	1-2
Chervil	1 Bunch	Cherry tomatoes	1 punnet
		Marjoram	1 bunch finely chopped
		Olive oil	10mls
		Orange juice	30mls

Method:

1. Dice chicken breast and skewer leave to the side
2. Get a bowl chop garlic, lemon juice salt/pepper, finely chop chervil put into the bowl then pour over the chicken leave to the side
3. Prepare salad peel and chop pumpkin roast for 15 mins or until ¾ cooked in the oven on a tray covered with foil at 160*C
4. Cook chicken in fry pan
5. Prepare rest of salad ingredients get a halve the cherry tomatoes put rocket, walnuts, olive oil, salt/ pepper, orange juice, cut apples any way you like
6. Finely chop Marjoram put in bowl and then add pumpkin toss and put to the side
7. At this point your chicken skewers should be ready get a plate put salad, chicken skewers on eat and enjoy

Satay chicken stir-fry with rice

Chicken breast	1-4 pieces
Rice	1 cup (250grms) will feed 3 people
Capsicum	1 choose any colour
Onion (brown)	1
Mushrooms (flat)	3
Bean shoots	1 bag

Sauce:

Peanut butter	200grms
Garlic	5 cloves
Tumerick	pinch
Ginger	10grms
Lemon grass	½ stalk
Water	300mls

Method:

1. In a saucepan put peanut butter, chop Garlic, Tumerick, Ginger Lemon Grass, water leave on stove low heat until you have cooked the rest stir occasionally
2. Let water come to the boil in a pot and cook rice for 15 mins
3. Dice chicken breast put to the side
4. Cut capsicum, onion, mushrooms leave mushrooms bean shoots to the side
5. Cook onion, capsicum until they are translucent put to the side
6. Cook chicken
7. Cook mushrooms, bean shoots
8. Add onion, capsicum and then add the sauce
9. Then get a plate and serve and enjoy

Mango chicken with seasonal vegetables

Chicken breast	1
Pumpkin	¼
Onion	1
Capsicum	1
Bean shoots	¼ of a bag
Mushrooms	8 small

Sauce:

Orange	1
Mango	1
Salt/ pepper	pinch
Garlic	5 cloves
Lemon Thyme	¼ bunch

Method:

1. Peel and cut pumpkin and put in the oven on a tray cover with foil at 160*C for 15 mins or until soft.
2. Prepare all sauce ingredients and put into a blender blend then put into a small saucepan heat on low then leave it. Once it's bubbling that's when it's ready to come off heat and then put to the side.
3. Cut chicken however way you and cook in a fry pan on low heat put to side
4. Prepare the rest of the vegetables cook in order onion, capsicum, mushrooms, bean shoots.
5. Add sauce and pumpkin to the vegetables.
6. Get a plate put vegetables on add your chicken eat and yum!

December 29, 2019 92KG still the same height I have found since I've had the surgery I plateau a lot more frequently than someone who hasn't had the surgery. So after getting my tubes tied, I made a decision a long time ago after two very different and terrifying pregnancy, I decided I didn't want to be pregnant anymore as I wasn't put on this earth to breed. I was destined to do great things and try and build a business for myself. There is one other major surgery I've got to complete and that is a tummy tuck, I think I might do it when

Here is a picture of me at size 18.

Decoeta is less dependent on me and when she is a bit easier to manage. I've had an exciting and terrifying year at the same time. With the new year starting afresh with what I've been through I hope that somewhere out there someone can draw strength by reading this story, have the courage to go for their dreams no matter what obstacles stand in their way and don't be afraid to over-come them head on. Mayson, Craig, and Decoeta they are my past, present and future and have made a significant impact on my life. With Decoeta being the newest addition, I advocate for being a healthy weight, I don't think I would have got there without the help of the surgery and without the support of my husband for me to feel better about myself and not hate myself. I had to go to the extreme which I'm glad I did. Otherwise I would have been over 200KG and six feet under.

Here is a picture of me at size 16.

So with me trying to move to the next phase of my business and that is stepping out of my comfort zone and going that little bit further of actually owning a premises that is not at home, I'm ready to take that next phase into the future with nothing stopping me The end is only the beginning.

Then fast forward to 1/1/2020 Happy New years at size 14

Printed in the United States
By Bookmasters